AUTHENTIC GUITAR TAB EDITION

MW01013025

Stefan Grossman's
EARLY MASTERS
of AMERICAN
BLUES GUITAR

DELTA BLUES GUITAR

EDITED AND TRANSCRIBED BY STEFAN GROSSMAN

Cover photo courtesy of Don Schlitten.
Interior photos, unless otherwise noted, are courtesy of Stefan Grossman.

Alfred Publishing Co., Inc.
16320 Roscoe Blvd., Suite 100
P.O. Box 10003
Van Nuys, CA 91410-0003
alfred.com

ISBN-10: 0-7390-4280-7 (Book & CD)
ISBN-13: 978-0-7390-4280-9 (Book & CD)

INTRODUCTION

by Stefan Grossman

*"There are fashions in music as in anything else, and folk-song presents no exception to the rule.
(For the last several years the most popular type of Negro song has been that peculiar, barbaric sort of melody called 'blues', with its irregular rhythm, its lagging briskness, its mournful liveliness of tone.) It has a jerky tempo, as of a cripple dancing because of some irresistible impulse. A 'blues' (or does one say a 'blue'? What is the grammar of the thing?) likes to end its stanza abruptly, leaving the listener expectant for more—though, of course, there is no fixed law about it. One could scarcely imagine a convention of any kind in connection with this Negroid free music. It is partial to the three-line stanza instead of the customary one of four or more, though not insisting on it, and it ends with a high note that has the effect of incompleteness. The close of a stanza comes with a shock like the whip-crack surprise at the end of an O. Henry story, for instance—a cheap trick, but effective as a novelty. It sings of themes remote from those of the old spirituals, and its incompleteness of stanza makes the listener gasp, and perhaps fancy that the censor had deleted the other line."*

— published 1915: *On the Trail of Negro Folk Songs*, Dorothy Scarborough

I have been playing the guitar for years. I started at the age of nine and by the time I reached fifteen I was studying with Rev. Gary Davis, one of the greatest exponents of fingerstyle blues and gospel guitar playing. Over the last forty years of studying, teaching, composing and writing, I still find my musical interests centered around a type of music classified as the Blues.

Much has been written about the story of the blues and its lyrical content. Without doubt, the blues hold a vital story of an oppressed people. Its lyrics are an American form of poetry at its finest. Its influence can be felt in classical compositions as well as to the most avant garde pieces of "sound music." Everyday we are bombarded by segments of the blues story that have permeated into the mainstream of today's pop music.

My interest for blues has always centered around the guitar. The sounds of blues guitar, whether finger-picked, flatpicked, played with a bottleneck, played on the guitarist's lap or strummed simply, has always intrigued me. My first encounter with blues music came via a Folkways Record of Big Bill Broonzy. I suppose the high powered voice of Big Bill combined with his exciting guitar playing was enough to capture the spirit of any young "city-billy" trying to learn how to tackle those six strings on his newly acquired guitar.

I spent several months buying records that featured Black men holding guitars. I was not familiar with the many names of bluesmen and could only use the album covers as my guide. I soon discovered names like Blind Lemon Jefferson, Blind Blake, Son House, Charlie Patton, Lightnin' Hopkins, Howlin' Wolf, Muddy Waters, Mississippi John Hurt, Elizabeth Cotten, and Rev. Gary Davis. The names in themselves held enough attraction for me. Their music was something else completely. Every record produced a new and profound listening experience. I became obsessed to hear *all* the new and old blues records.

As this was happening, I had the fortune to meet and study under Rev. Gary Davis. He patiently taught me many of the marvels of blues guitar playing. I was indeed very fortunate in finding Rev. Davis as here was a great bluesman that was also a self-acclaimed teacher. He thrived on teaching interested students and he himself had mastered many guitar techniques and styles of other musicians. Rev. Davis was unique in this respect. Firstly, he was a teacher and had shown many famous blues musicians how to play (this list is a long one and contains Blind Boy Fuller, Brownie McGee, Larry Johnson, Ry Cooder, Dave Bromberg and many others). Secondly, he differed from other bluesmen in that he had perfected and studied many styles. He could play one tune in a variety of ways and follow the development of that song from Texas, to Mississippi, to the Carolinas, to the northern cities and then back. It was from Rev. Davis that I became aware of the regional blues styles that the Black bluesmen had developed in America.

During the same period, friends of mine were hitting the highways trying to rediscover "legendary" names. Skip James, Bukka White, Son House and Mississippi John Hurt were being sought after. Within a one year period all of these men were found, recorded, and brought North to perform to eagerly awaiting audiences. The "blues revival" was in full swing. I started to interview and study with these musicians. I was trying to put pieces together in the jigsaw puzzle of blues guitar styles.

This collection presents a wide variety of wonderful Mississippi Delta blues arrangements. You should have fun tackling the arrangements of Son House, Skip James, Willie Brown, Arthur Pettis and Charlie Patton. It is fundamental in your understanding of these arrangements to hear the original performances which we have included on the CD that accompanies this book.

My thanks to Jas Obrect and Mark Humphrey for writing the biographical sketches of each bluesman. The stories of these great men are intertwined with their music.

Enjoy and if you have any questions or suggestions you can contact me via www.guitarvideos.com.

Keep picking,

EXPLANATION OF THE TAB/MUSIC SYSTEM

"…Learning from listening is unquestionably the best way, the only way that suits this kind of music. You are setting the notes down for a record of what happened, a record that can be studied, preserved and so on, a necessary and useful companion to the recordings of the actual sounds. I keep thinking of this as I transcribe; if you could do it, it would be good to have a legend across each page reading: 'Listen to the record if you want to learn the song.'"

—Hally Wood (taken from the Publisher's Foreword to the *New Lost City Ramblers Songbook*.)

These words are most suitable for introducing the tablature system, for tablature is just a guide and should be used in conjunction with the recordings. Tablature is not like music notation, however the combination of TAB and music in an arrangement forms a complete language. Used together with the original recordings, they give a total picture of the music.

The TAB system does not attempt to show rhythms or accents. These can be found on the music or heard in the recordings. Music notation tackles these articulations to a degree, but the overall sensations, the feel and the soul of music cannot be wholly captured on the written page. In the words of the great Sufi Hazrat Inayat Khan, "…the traditional ancient songs of India composed by great Masters have been handed down from father to son. The way music is taught is different from the Western way. It is not always written, but is taught by imitation. The teacher sings and the pupil imitates and the intricacies and subtleties are learned by imitation."

This is the theme I've tried to interpolate into the tablature. Tablature is the roadmap and you are the driver. Now to the TAB.

Each space indicates a string. The top space represents the first string, second space the second string, etc. A zero means an open string, a number in the space indicates the fretted position, for instance a 1 in a space indicates the first fret of that string.

In the diagram below, the zero is on the second string and indicates the open second string is played. The 1 is placed on the third string and signifies the first fret of the third string. Likewise, the 4 is in the fourth space and indicates the fourth fret of the fourth string.

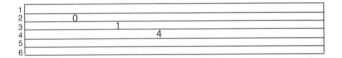

Generally, for fingerpicking styles you will be playing the thumb, index, and middle fingers of your picking hand. To indicate the picking finger in TAB, the stems go up and line up down from the numbers.

A. A stem down means that your thumb strikes the note.

B. If a stem is up, your index or middle finger strikes the note. The choice of finger is left up to you, as your fingers will dictate what is most comfortable, especially when playing a song up to tempo!

C. The diagram below shows an open sixth string played with the thumb followed by the second fret of the third string played with the index or middle finger:

In most cases, the thumb will play an alternating bass pattern, usually on the bass strings. The index and middle fingers play melodic notes on the first, second and third strings. Please remember, this is not a rule; there are many exceptions.

In fingerpicking there are two "picking" styles: regular picking and "pinching" two notes together. A pinch is shown in the TAB by a line connecting two notes. A variation of this can also be two treble notes pinched with a bass note. Follow the examples below from left to right.

1) The open sixth string is played with the thumb.

2) The first fret of the sixth string is pinched together with the third fret on the third string. The sixth string is played with the thumb, the third string with the index finger.

3) The thumb strikes the third fret of the fourth string.

4) The first fret/sixth string is played with the thumb; it's pinched with two notes in the treble. The index and middle fingers strike the first fret/first string and the third fret/second string.

5) The next note is the index finger hitting the first fret/second string.

6) Lastly, the bass note is played with the thumb on the third fret/fourth string.

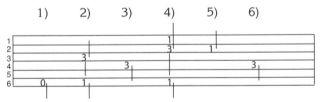

There are certain places in blues and contemporary guitar that call for the use of either strumming techniques or accented bass notes. The TAB illustrates these as follows:

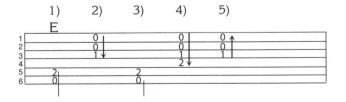

1) The thumb hits the open sixth string and the second fret on the fifth string should also sound. For example, play an E chord. Now strike the open string and vary the force of your attack. Try hitting it hard enough so that the fifth string vibrates as well. This technique is very important for developing a full sound and the right alternating bass sound.

2) Next, the arrow notation indicates a brush and the arrowhead indicates the direction of the brush.

   A. If the arrowhead is pointed down, the hand brushes up towards the sixth string.

   B. If pointed up, the hand brushes down towards the first string.

   C. The number of strings to be played by the brush is shown by the length of the arrows. For example, this arrow shows a brush up toward the sixth string, but indicates to strike only the first, second and third strings.

   D. The brush can be done with your whole hand, index finger or middle and ring finger. Let comfort plus a full and "right" sound guide your choice.

3) The third set of notes again shows the sixth string/open bass note played with the thumb and being struck hard enough to make the fifth string/second fretted position sound.

4) Once more, an arrow pointed downward indicates a brush up. This example forms an E chord and the brush up includes the first, second, third, and fourth strings.

5) The last set of notes has an arrow pointed upward, indicating a brush downward striking the first, second, and third strings.

Here are several special effects that are also symbolized in tablature:

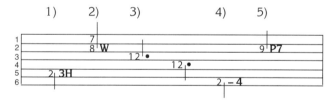

1) HAMMER-ON: Designated by an "H" which is placed after the stem on the fret to be hammered. In the example above, fret the second fret/fifth string and pick it with your thumb. Then "hammer-on" (hit hard) the third fret/fifth string (i.e., fret the third fret/fifth string). This is an all-in-one, continuous motion which will produce two notes rapidly with one picking finger strike.

2) WHAM: Designated by a "W." In the example the eighth fret/second string is "whammed" and played with the seventh fret/first string. Both notes are played together with your index and middle fingers respectively. The whammed note is "stretched." We do this by literally bending the note up. We can "wham" the note up a half tone, full tone, etc.

3) HARMONICS: Symbolized by a dot (•). To play a harmonic, gently lay your finger directly above the indicated fret (don't press down!) The two notes in the example are both harmonics. The first on the twelfth fret/third string is played with the index/middle finger, while the second note—twelfth fret/fourth string—is played with the thumb.

4) SLIDE: Shown with a dash (–). Play the second fret/sixth string and then slide up to the fourth fret of the sixth string. This is a continuous movement, the string is struck once with your thumb.

5) PULL-OFF: "P" designates a "pull-off." Fret both the seventh and ninth frets on the second string. Play the ninth fret with your index/middle finger and then quickly remove it in the same stroke, leaving the seventh fret/second string. Pull-offs are generally in a downward direction.

6) In certain cases, other specific symbols are added to the TAB:

   A. For ARTIFICIAL HARMONICS, an "X" is placed after the fretted position.

   B. For SNAPPING, a note an indication may be given with a symbol or the written word.

Many times, these special techniques are combined. For instance, putting a pull-off and a hammer-on together. Coordination of your fretting and picking hands will be complex initially, but the end results are exciting and fun to play.

PICKING HAND POSITION FOR FINGERPICKING STYLES

The Classical and Flamenco schools have strict right-hand rules, however for this style of acoustic fingerpicking, there are no rules, only suggestions. Your right hand position should be dictated by comfort, however in observation of many well-known fingerpickers, I found one hand position similarity—they all tend to rest their little finger and/or ring finger on the face of the guitar. This seems to help their balance for accenting notes and control of the guitar. Experiment with this position, it may feel uncomfortable at first. I ask my students to perfect this position and then compare the sound to when their finger(s) were not placed on the face of the guitar. They usually find the sound is greatly improved when some contact is kept with the guitar face.

MUSIC NOTATION

We have somewhat adapted the music notation in that this also shows whether the note is picked with your thumb or index/middle fingers. The stems of the music notes correspond to the direction of the TAB stems. I hope this will make the music notation clearer to fingerpicking guitarists.

I hope you will feel at home and comfortable with the tablature and musical notations. Remember, these are only road maps indicating where and how you should place your fingers. The playing and musical interpretation is up to you.

WILLIE BROWN

"The possibilities of the phonograph in these studies indicate one of the great advantages of this instrument...The collector may not have a musical ear...and may not be able to write out the songs, no matter how many times they are repeated. He can, in that case, submit them at some favorable time to one who is able to catch the song and set it to music."

—Ethnologist Jesse Walter Fewkes, *Science*, May 2, 1890

Today we can scarcely imagine a work without recorded sound, or both how revolutionary and magical the Edison cylinder was when it appeared in 1877. Social scientists who sought to document the aural artifacts (i.e. languages and music) of endangered cultures quickly realized what an invaluable tool had come into their hands. Ethnologist Jesse Walter Fewkes made the very first "field recordings" in 1890 of Passamaquoddy Indians in Calais, Maine. Similar recordings of African-American folksong began sometime before World War I, and accelerated in the 1930s.

The notion of scouring the rural South of half a century ago for remnants of older songs and musical styles is undeniably romantic, but it was also a difficult task. For one thing, the goals of the folklorist, to collect "specimens" for study, and the goals of the folklorist's "informant" (singer-musician) were sometimes at odds, especially if the informant had prior experience with commercial recordings. Son House recalled with mixed amusement and consternation how he sang long and hard in the hot Mississippi summer for Alan Lomax, and the extent of his payment was a Coca-Cola ("But it was a cold one," House added).

Alan Lomax and his father John made some of the most extraordinary "finds" of any folklorists. In 1933, they found Leadbelly at the Louisiana State Penitentiary at Angola. In a collaborative field trip sponsored by the Library of Congress and Fisk University in 1941, Alan Lomax and John W. Work found a stunning young blues singer, McKinley Morganfield, on Stovall's Plantation in Mississippi. He was also known as Muddy Waters, and suggested that folklorists seek out the man from whom Waters had learned so much, Son House. Years later, Walters said of Lomax, "Really, what he was looking for was Robert Johnson, but Robert had got killed."

Lomax and Work had stumbled onto the most influential Delta bluesmen of the post-War era and his mentor, one of the greats of the previous generation. Even if the gravity of those appearances would not be apparent for some years, Lomax and Work knew they had struck paydirt, and were back for more the following summer. There would be further recordings of Waters and House, and of such Robert Johnson cohorts as David "Honeyboy" Edwards. In 1942, there would also be tantalizing obscurities like William Brown, recorded at Sadie Beck's Plantation in Arkansas. Brown recorded three fine blues ("Mississippi Blues," "East St. Louis Blues," and "Ragged and Dirty"), and accompanied the eccentric Willie "61" Blackwell on such titles as the Nipponophobic "Junior, a Jap's Girl Christmas for His Santa Claus." Though Blackwell was rediscovered in Detroit in the '60s, no one seems to have inquired about his 1942 accompanist and Brown, like many fine but sparsely recorded bluesmen, remains a mystery.

In the notes to the album, Walking Blues (Flyright FY LP 541), John H. Cowley wrote: "Nothing is known of Blackwell's guitar-playing companion William Brown (not the same man as Willie Brown), excepting that in a few comments following Brown's recording of 'East St. Louis Blues' (AFS 6606 A 2) he sounds an older man than Blackwell; a fact born out by Lomax asking Brown whether he knew any pre-blues like 'Stagolee' and 'Railroad Bill,' both of which William had 'forgotten.'"

One of Brown's recorded songs was a blues of rare vintage, according to W.C. Handy's autobiographical Father of the Blues: "While sleeping on the cobblestones in St. Louis (1892), I heard shabby guitarists picking out a tune called 'East St. Louis.' It had numerous one-line verses and they would sing it all night." But of William Brown we know no more than we do of the "shabby guitarrists" who, Handy wrote, "may well have contributed to my writing the 'St. Louis Blues'..."

Future Blues

as performed by Willie Brown

Open G Tuning: DGDGBD

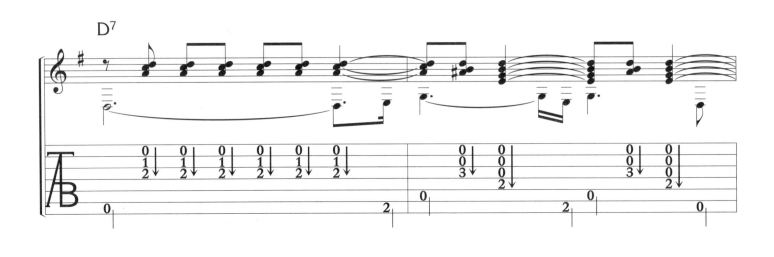

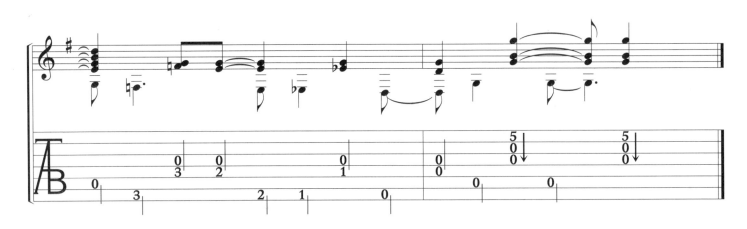

Future Blues
Lead Sheet

2. The min - utes seem like ho - urs an' ho - urs seem like days,

An' the min - utes seem like ho - urs,

ho - urs seem like days, An' it seems

like my wom-an ought - a stop her low - down ways.

1. Can't tell my future, honey, I can't tell my past.
   Lord, it seems like every minute sure gonna be my last.

2. The minutes seems like hours, an' hours seems like days,
   An' the minutes seems like hours, hours seems like days.
   An' it seems like my woman oughta stop her low-down way.

3. Lord, the woman I love, now she's five feet from the ground,
   I says, woman I love, mama, is five feet from the ground.
   And she's tailor-made and ain't no hand-me-down.

4. Lord, and I got a woman now, Lordie, she lightnin' when she,
   lightnin' when she, lightnin' smiles.
   I says, I've got a woman, Lord, she lightnin' when she smiles.
   Five feet and four inches, and she's just good huggin' size.

5. Girl, I know you see that picture now, Lordie, up,
   up on your mother's, up on your mother's, mama' shelf?
   I know, you see that picture, Lord, up on your motherin' shelf?
   Girl, you know by that I'm gettin' tired o' sleepin' by myself.

6. And it's "T" for Texas, now, and it's "T" for Tennessee,
   And it's "T" for Texas, Lord, it's "T" for Tennessee.
   Lord bless that woman that put the thing on me.

M&O Blues

as performed by Willie Brown

Standard Tuning

M&O Blues

Lead Sheet

1.   I leaves here I'm gonna catch that M and O,
     Now when I leave here I'm gonna catch that M and O,
     I'm goin' way down south where (it) ain't never been this slow.

2.   'Cause I had a notion, Lord, and I believe I will,
     'Cause I had a notion, Lord, and I believe I will,
     I'm gonna build me a mansion out on Decatur hill.

3.   Now, it's all o' you men, oughta be 'shamed of yourself,
     And it's all o' you men, oughta be 'shamed of yourself,
     Goin' round here swearin' 'fore God you got a poor woman by yourself.

4.   I started to kill my woman till she laid down 'cross the bed,
     I started to kill my woman till, laid down 'cross the bed,
     And she looked so ambitious till I took back everything I said.

5.   And I asked her, "How 'bout it?" Lord, and she said, "All right."
     And I asked her, "How 'bout it?" Lord, and she said, "All right."
     But she never showed up at the shack last night,

     And she...

Ragged and Dirty

Standard Tuning

as performed by Willie Brown

Ragged and Dirty
Lead Sheet

Lord, I'm ___ broke ___ and I'm hun - gry, ragged and dirt - y too. ___

Broke and hun - gry, ___ rag - ged and

dirt - y too. ___ If I clean up sweet

ma - ma to night, ___ stay all night ___ with you? ___

1. Lord, I'm broke and I'm hungry, ragged and dirty too.
   Broke and I'm hungry, ragged and dirty too.I
   If I clean up sweet mama, (can I) stay all night with you?

2. Lord, I went to my window, baby, I couldn't see through my blinds.
   Went to my window, baby, couldn't see through my blinds.
   Heard my best friend a-comin' now, thought I heard my baby cryin'.

3. Lord, if I can't come in, baby, just let me sit down in your door.
   I can't come in, baby, let me sit down in your door.
   And I will leave so soon that your man won't ever know.

4. Lord, how can I live here, baby, Lord, I feel at ease.
   How can I live here, baby, Lord, I feel at ease,
   'Cause that woman that I got, man, she do just what she feel.

5. Lord, you shouldn't mistreat me, baby, because I'm young and wild.
   Shouldn't mistreat me because I'm young and wild.
   You must always remember baby you was once a child.

6. Lord, I'm leavin' in the morning, baby, if I have to ride the blinds.
   Leavin' in the morning, have to ride the blinds.
   Been (mis)treated, baby, and I swear I don't mind dying.

SON HOUSE

In the years before World War II, Son House created some of the purest, most powerful Mississippi Delta blues on record. Playing partners with Charlie Patton and Willie Brown, he exerted a profound influence on Robert Johnson and Muddy Waters, both of whom copied his music and carried it to new generations. House's influence still echoes through the Rolling Stones, Eric Clapton, and many other musicians. In many respects, Son House is the true father of what's known today as "deep blues."

Eddie James "Son" House was born a couple of miles outside of Clarksdale, Mississippi, on March 21, 1902. A "churchified" field worker in his youth, Son preached his first sermon at 15. Willie Wilson, an unrecorded bottleneck player, inspired him to take up slide guitar and taught him to tune to an open chord. House learned to match thumbed bass notes with treble slides and was soon playing local juke joints. Another local musician, James McCoy, taught him fingerstyle arrangements of "My Black Mama" and "Preaching the Blues," which Son adapted for bottleneck.

In 1928, House shot a man, pled self-defense, and was convicted of manslaughter. A judge reviewing the case freed him two years later and House hotfooted it to Lula, Mississippi, where he teamed with Charlie Patton, the Delta's most famous bluesman, and Willie Brown. In May 1930, the trio journeyed to Grafton, Wisconsin, to record for Paramount. Son inaugurated his recording career with "My Black Mama," "Preachin' the Blues," "Clarksdale Moan," "Dry Spell Blues," and other classic examples of the early Delta blues style. House's next sessions, for the Library of Congress in 1941 and 1942, featured him as both a solo artist and with a countrified band. With his superb vocals and sure-handed bottleneck, Son was at the peak of his powers, but his performance only netted him a Coca-Cola.

Around 1943, Son House moved to Rochester, New York, and took a job as a rivet heater for the New York Central Railroad dispatch shop. After the war he was promoted to porter and assigned the Empire State Express run to Chicago, a job he held for more than decade. When he got word in 1952 that his old playing pal Willie Brown had died, House "went right," quit playing blues, and joined the Amen Baptist Church.

With the resurgence of interest in blues music in the early 1960s, Son was located by blues 78 collectors Dick Waterman, Phil Spiro, and Nick Perls. His rediscovery was trumpeted in *Newsweek*, and with Waterman as his manager, House was soon playing festivals and making albums. To alleviate tremors and quell his nervousness, Son, deeply alcoholic, often downed double shots of gin or bourbon. On stage and record, though, he emerged as a passionate performer with a self-effacing personality. For a few years House toured extensively and recorded for Blue Goose, Vanguard, Verve/Folkways, Liberty, and other labels. Deteriorating health forced his retirement in 1976, and he spent his final years living with his family in Highland Park, Michigan. On October 19, 1988, the last of the great first-generation Delta singers died in his sleep at Detroit's Harper Hospital.

Recorded in open G, Son House's two-part "My Black Mama" endures as one of the essential prewar Delta blues performances. Recorded for Paramount in May 1930, the song influenced Robert Johnson, who recycled its riff in "Walking Blues," and Muddy Waters, who recast is as "Country Blues." Son played the song by waving his arm up and down in a long arc, thumbing the bass strings on the down swoop and plucking the slide lick with his index finger on the way back up. Watch a video of Son House to see the all-important role his body movement played in his driving style.

Recorded for Paramount at the May 1930 session, Son House's "Dry Spell Blues" gave a gripping account of a disastrous drought. Like "My Black Mama," it was originally issued as a two-part 78. The song uses a melody common to Willie Brown's "M&O Blues" and parts of Charley Patton's "Pony Blues." An extremely physical guitarist, House not only kept time with his left foot and swinging right arm, but his whole being—his head, neck, shoulders, and all the rest—seemed to vibrate in the rhythm of his song.

Dry Spell Blues, Part One

as performed by Son House

Open G Tuning: DGDGBD

Dry Spell Blues, Part One

Lead Sheet

Them dry spell blues have caused— me to drift from door to———— door,-

— Dry spell blues have caused— me

to drift from door to————— door,— These dry spell blues have put ev' - ry -

bod - y on the kil - lin'———— floor.—

1. Them dry spell blues have caused me to drift from door to door,
   Dry spell blues have caused me to drift from door to door,
   These dry spell blues have put everybody on the killin' floor.

2. Now, the people down South, soon won't have no home.
   Oh Lord, the people down South, soon won't have no home.
   'Cause this dry spell has parched all this cotton and corn.

3. Now I fold my arms and I walked away.
   Now I fold my arms, Lord I walked away.
   Just like I tell you, somebody's got to pray.

4. Pork chops 45 cents a pound, cotton is only 10.
   Pork chops 45 cents a pound, cotton is only 10.
   I can't keep no women, no no never did.

5. So dry old bo'weevil, turned up his toes and die.
   So dry old bo'weevil, turned up his toes and die.
   Now nothing to do, make moonshine and rye.

My Black Mama, Part One

as performed by Son House

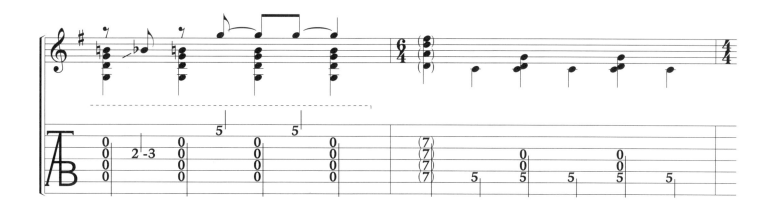

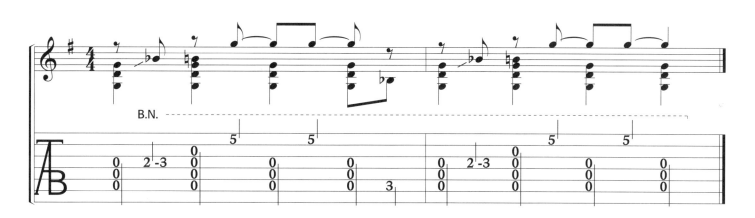

My Black Mama, Part One
Lead Sheet

Oh, oh,_____ black ma - ma what's the mat - ter with you,_____ well it ain't sat - is - fac - t'ry, don't care what I do,_____ Yeah, black ma - ma what's the mat - ter with you,_____ Well it ain't sat - is - fac - t'ry ba - by, don't care what I__ do._____

1. Oh, oh, black mama, what's the matter with you?
    Well it ain't satisfactory, don't care what I do.
    Yeah, black mama, what's the matter with you?
    Well it ain't satisfactory, baby, don't care what I do.

2. You take a brownskin woman'll make a rabbit move to town,
    Say, but a jet-black woman'll make a mule kick his stable down.
    Oh, a brownskin woman'll make a rabbit move to town,
    Oh, but a real black woman'll make a mule kick his stable down.

3. Say, 'tain't no heaven, say, there ain't no burnin' hell,
    Say where I'm goin' when I die, can't nobody tell.
    Oh there ain't no heaven, now, there ain't no burnin' hell,
    Oh, where I'm goin' when I die, can't nobody tell.

4. Well, my black mama's face shine like the sun,
    Oh, lipstick and powder sure won't help her none.
    My black mama's face shine like the sun,
    Oh, lipstick and powder, well, they sure won't help her none.

5. Well, you see my milk cow, tell her to hurry home,
    I ain't had no milk since that cow been gone.
    If you see my milk cow, tell her to hurry home,
    Yeah, I ain't had no milk since that cow been gone.

6.   Well, I'm goin' to the racetrack to see my pony run,
      He ain't the best in the world, but he's a runnin' son-of-a-gun.
      I'm goin' to the racetrack to see my pony run,
      He ain't the best in the world, but he's a runnin' son-of-a-gun.

7.   Oh, Lord have mercy on my wicked soul,
      Wouldn't mistreat you, baby, for my weight in gold.
      Oh, Lord have mercy on my wicked soul,
      (Last line hummed).

Part Two

1.   Hey, I solemnly swear, Lord, I raise my right hand,
      That I'm gonna get me a woman, you can get you another man.
      I solemnly swear, Lord, I raise my right hand,
      That I'm gonna get me a woman, babe, you can get you another man.

2.   I got a letter this mornin', how do you think it read?
      "Oh, hurry, hurry, the gal you love is dead."
      I got a letter this mornin', how do your reckon it read?
      "Oh, hurry, hurry, the gal you love is dead."

3.   I grabbed my suitcase, I took off up the road,
      I got there, she was layin' on the coolin' board.
      I grabbed my suitcase, I took on up the road,
      Oh, when I got there, she was layin' on the coolin' board.

4.   Well I walked up close, I looked down in her face,
      Good old gal, you got to lay here till Judgement Day.
      I walked up close, and I looked down in her face,
      Yes, been a good old gal, got to lay here till Judgment Day.

Spoken:

Aw sho' now, I feel low-down this evenin'!

5.   Oh, my woman so black, she stays apart of this town,
      Can't nothin' "go" when the poor gal is around
      My black mama stays apart of this town,
      Oh, can't nothin' "go" when the poor gal is around.

6.   Oh, some people tell me the worried blues ain't bad,
      It's the worst old feelin' that I ever had.
      Some people tell me the worried blues ain't bad,
      Buddy, the worst old feelin', Lord, I ever had.

7.   Mmm, I fold my arms, and I walked away,
      "That's all right, mama, your trouble will come someday."
      I fold my arms, Lord, I walked away,
      Say, "that's all right, mama, your trouble will come someday."

SKIP JAMES

He may have been from the same Mississippi Delta region that bred Tommy Johnson, Ishman Bracey, Charlie McCoy, and the Mississippi Sheiks, but Skip James had a style and personality all his own. Aloof and enigmatic, he always performed solo and mostly kept to himself. Played on guitar or piano, his songs are among the most intense—and inspirational—blues on record.

Born on the Whitehead Plantonia in Betonia, Missisippi, in 1902, Nehemiah "Skip" James learned guitar as a boy, developing a very personal, introverted blues style accentuated by an eerie, high-pitched falsetto. He played most songs in a "cross-note" (or E minor) tuning of E, B, E, G, B, E, but also knew how to play in standard tuning and open G. In his twenties, James moved to Jackson, Mississippi. His only prewar recording session, held in Grafton, Wisconsin, in February 1931, produced 11 classic guitar blues—his strikingly beautiful "Devil Got My Woman," "Hard Time Killing Floor," "I'm So Glad," and "Cherry Ball Blues" among them—as well as the gospel songs "Be Ready When He Comes" and "Jesus Is a Mighty Good Leader." On these sides Skip's clean fingerpicking provided a perfect complement to his high-pitched vocals. James added to the music's considerable tension by launching into uncommon single-string embellishments. Skip finished the Grafton session with five unique piano blues featuring cascades of notes careening into sudden pauses.

For a while during the early 1930s, James played blues around Jackson, working the same venues as Johnny Temple and Little Brother Montgomery. He then dropped out of what he described as "music racket." He attended a Baptist seminary, became a preacher, and toured with gospel groups and jubilee singers. Meanwhile, Johnny Temple, who learned the E-minor tuning from Skip James, showed Robert Johnson the "Devil Got My Woman" pattern, which Robert transformed into "Hell Hound on My Trail." Skip's "22-20 Blues," recorded on piano, was recast by Johnson as "32-20 Blues."

During the 1940s, James reportedly lived with his father, a Baptist minister, in Plano, Texas. He returned to Mississippi in the early 1950s. In 1963, acting on a tip from Bukka White, young white musicians John Fahey, Bill Barth, and Henry

Vestine found Skip James in the Tunica County Hospital, convalescing from a stomach disorder. When he was well enough to perform, James began recording again and became a favorite at folk and blues festivals. He also became something of a mentor to struggling guitarists, who described him as being intense and almost professorial about his music. In 1967, Eric Clapton and Jack Bruce introduced Skip's music to millions of rock fans by transforming "I'm So Glad" into a staple at Cream concerts. The royalties helped Skip pay for his mounting medical expenses. Suffering from cancer, Skip James passed away in Philadelphia in 1969. During the ensuing years, his style has reverberated through Bowling Green John Cephus's remarkably close covers, as well as in the styles of Bentonia-based bluesmen such as Jack Owens and Bud Spires.

Skip James's dark, foreboding signature song, "Devil Got My Woman" has few parallels in blues—Robert Johnson's "Hell Hound on My Trail" is its nearest equivalent. Skip reportedly wrote the two-chord song when his short-lived marriage to a preacher's daughter ended with her running away with another man. Skip played it in open E-minor tuning at his February 1931 session for Paramount. James re-recorded a less-harrowing version of the song in 1964 at Adelphi Studios. Our transcription presents the superior Paramount version.

Stark and unrepentant, this dirge-like masterpiece "Hard Time Killin' Floor," uses the hardship of the Depression to delve deep into the heart of the blues: "Times is harder than ever before." Skip's moaning vocals sound African in origin, while his fingerpicked figures, sonic evidence suggests, are played close to the bridge. Again, James is playing in open E-minor tuning. Backed with "Cherry Ball Blues," this was the first Skip James record to be released.

Unlike most of Skip James's Paramount 78s, "Special Rider Blues" is played in open-G tuning. Skip's inspiration for the melody was pianist Little Brother Montgomery's "Vicksburg Blues," although decades later Skip qualified this by stating, "I just listened to a few of his notes." A "special rider," in the parlance of the day, was a lover. Notice how James uses unabashed solo flourishes to make his instrument "talk" after he finishes a vocal line. James himself described this as "a deep piece."

DEVIL GOT MY WOMAN

as performed by Skip James

Cross-Note Tuning – D minor: DADFAD

to Next Verse…

Devil Got My Woman

Lead Sheet

1. I'd rather be the devil than be that woman's man,
    I'd rather be the devil than be that woman's man.

2. I laid down last night, laid down last night.
    I laid down last night, tryin' to take my rest.
    My mind got to ramblin' like a wild geese from the west,
    From the west.

3. The woman I love, woman that I love,
    Woman I love, took her from my best friend.
    But he got lucky, took her back again.
    And he got lucky, took her back again.

Hard Time Killin' Floor

as performed by Skip James

Open E minor Tuning: EBEGBE

INTRO

GUITAR PART BEHIND MOAN in 1st VERSE

GUITAR PART BEHIND OTHER MOANS

TAG

Hard Time Killin' Floor
Lead Sheet

2. And the peo - ple are —— drift - in' —— from door to door, ——

Can't find no heav - en, I don't— care— where I go. ——

Hm—— hm—— hm—— hm—— Hm—— hm—— hm—— hm.

1.   Hard time here and everywhere you go,
    Times is harder than ever been before.

2.   And the people are driftin' from door to door
    Can't find no heaven, I don't care where I go.

3.   Hear me tell you people, just before I go,
    These hard times will kill you just dry long so.

4.   Well, you hear me singin' my (blue?) lonesome song,
    These hard times can last us so very long.

5.   If I ever get off this killin' floor,
    I'll never get down this low no more.
    No-no, no-no, I'll never get down this low no more.

6.   And you say you had money, you better be sure,
    'Cause these hard times will drive you from door to door.

7.   Sing this song and I ain't gonna sing no more,
    Sing this song and I ain't gonna sing no more.
    Hmm… Hard times will drive you from door to door.

SPECIAL RIDER

as performed by Skip James

Open G Tuning: DGDGBD

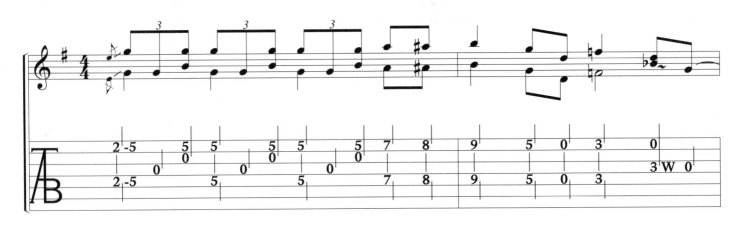

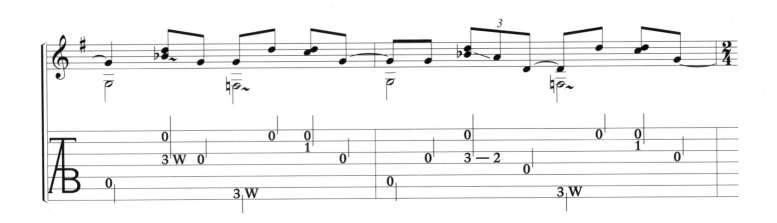

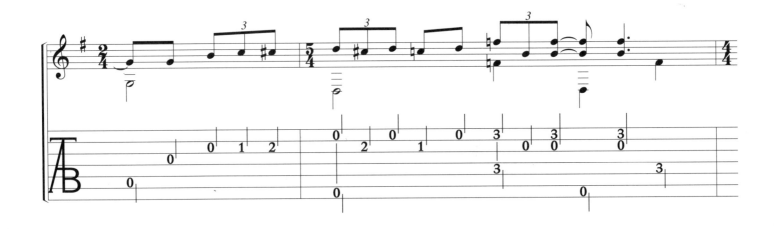

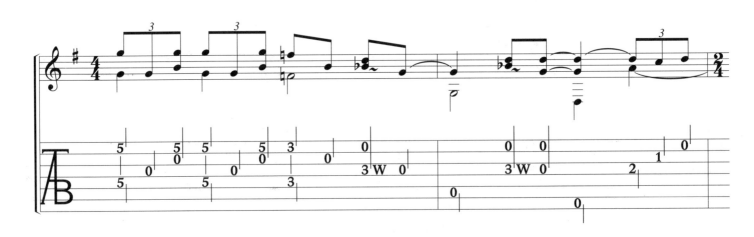

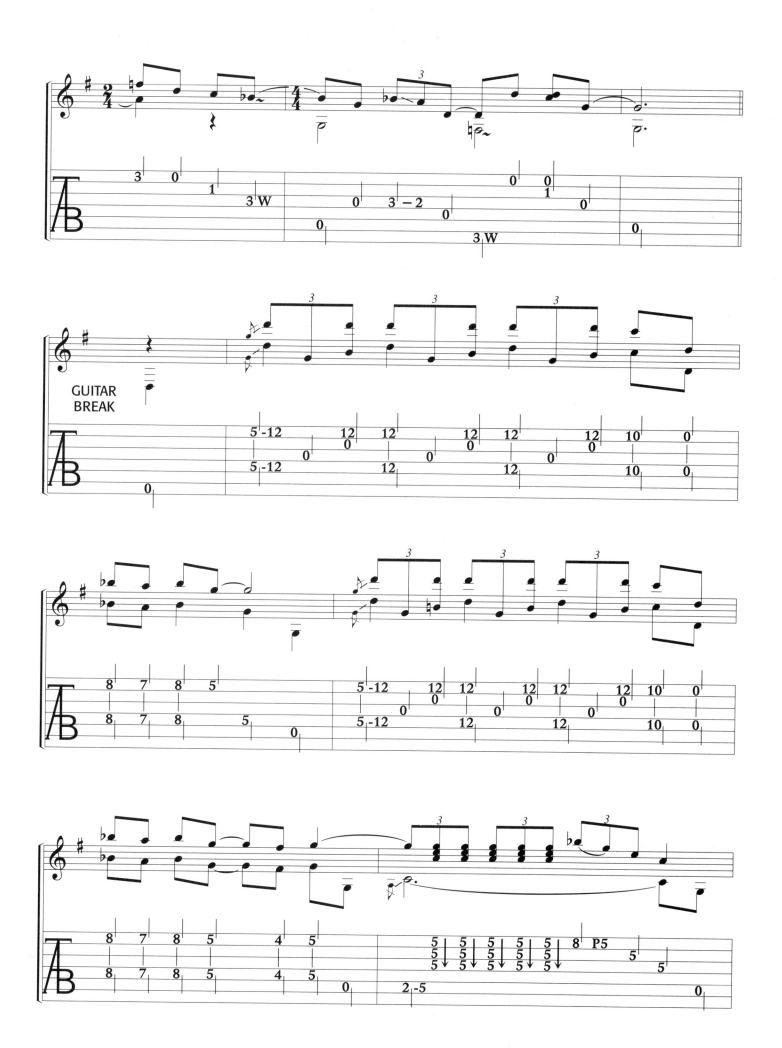

GUITAR
BREAK

Special Rider
Lead Sheet

I ain't got no ... spe - cial ri - der here,——

I ain't got no ... spe - cial ri - der here,

Ain't got no - bod - y to

love and feel—— my cares.——

1. I ain't got no special rider here,
   I ain't got no special rider here,
   Ain't got nobody to love and feel my cares.

2. I woke up this mornin', looked at the special risin' sun,
   Got up this morning, looked at the special risin' sun,
   Got up this mornin', looked at special risin' sun,
   An' I prayed to the Lord my special rider would go.

3. I sing this song to ease your trouble in mind,
   Sing this song, ease your trouble in mind,
   And you stay worried, yeah, and bothered all the time.

4. Hey, hey, what more can I do?
   Hey, hey, what more can I do?
   Honey, you must want me keep singin' these special blues.

1. I went to the river, couldn't get across.
   I jumped on your papa, 'cause I thought he was a horse now,
   Rode him over, give him Coca Cola, Lemon soda, saucer of ice cream,
   Take soap and water, for to keep it clean.

2. Up she jumped, down she fell,
   Her mouth flew open like a Mercury shell now,
   Got her over, give her Coca Cola, Lemon soda, saucer of ice cream,
   Take soap and water, for to keep it clean.

3. Your sister was a teddy, your daddy was a bear.
   Put the muzzle on your momma, 'cause you got bad hair now,
   Ride her over, give her Coca Cola, Lemon soda, saucer of ice cream,
   Take soap and water, for to keep it clean.

4. If you want to hear, now here's the last,
   Take him down to the river and wash his yas, yas, yas.
   Got him over, give him Coca Cola, Lemon soda, saucer of ice cream,
   Take soap and water, for to keep it clean.

5. If you want to go to heaven when you D.I.E.
   You got to put on your collar and your T.I.E. now
   Ride him over, give him Coca Cola, Lemon soda, saucer of ice cream,
   Take soap and water, for to keep it clean.

6. Now if you want to get the rabbit out of the L.O.G.
   You got to sit on the stump like the D.O.G. now
   Ride him over, give him Coca Cola, Lemon soda, saucer of ice cream,
   Take soap and water, for to keep it clean.

7. Run here doctor, run here fast See what's the matter with this yas, yas, yas.
   Rode him over, give him Coca Cola, Lemon soda, saucer of ice cream,
   Soap and water, for to keep it clean.

HAMBONE WILLIE NEWBERN

In March 1929, a field unit for OKeh Records set up shop in Atlanta, Georgia, to make records of the fiery gospel preacher J.M. Gates, Bessie Johnson's Sanctified Singers, vaudeville performer Cleo Gibson & Her Hot Three, the I.C. Glee Club Quartet, Sloppy Henry, the duo Tampa Joe and Macon Ed, and, appearing at his only session, Hambone Willie Newbern. Among the six titles Newbern recorded were "She Could Toodle-Oo,""Shelby County Workhouse Blues," "Hambone Willie's Dreamy-Eyed Woman's Blues," and what would ultimately become his enduring contribution to the blues, the first-ever recording of "Roll and Tumble Blues."

Playing with fingers and slide in open G, Newbern framed "Roll and Tumble Blues" as a dance tune, and it's likely that when he played it at gatherings, it extended beyond the three-minute limitation inherent in recording music onto one side of a 78 rpm record. Newbern, a subtle slider from rural Ripley, Tennessee, had apparently been playing the song for many years. Sleepy John Estes, who spent his childhood in Ripley, recalled hearing Newbern play the song between 1913 and 1917. It was likely a very common theme, and could well have been one of the earliest of all blues strains, perhaps even African in origin. The same year Newbern made his recording, Estes used the song's melody and "dough roller"

imagery for his debut recording, "The Girl I Love, She Got Long Curly Hair." Others, notably Furry Lewis, framed it as "Brownsville Blues."

Outside of his music, not much is known of Hambone Willie Newbern. Estes recalled taking guitar lessons from him and stated that they had played a medicine show together in Como, Mississippi. Newbern's brief recorded repertoire, which encompasses ragtime and "coon songs" as well as blues, supports the notion that he worked medicine shows. Sadly, Newbern was reportedly beaten to death in prison during the 1940s.

Within a few years of Newbern's original recording, the "Roll and Tumble" riff had become a staple of Mississippi Delta and Memphis blues. Robert Johnson revitalized the Newbern version for "If I Had Possession Over Judgment Day," climaxing his jacked-up arrangement with stratospheric slide. In 1948, Muddy Waters used the song as the basis for "Down South Blues," recorded for Aristocrat. A year later, he delivered a far more impassioned slide performance on Baby Face Leroy's "Rollin' and Tumblin', Part 1," one of the most unabashed postwar downhome blues records. To this day, the song is used by Mississippi artists such as R.L. Burnside to draw people onto the dance floor.

ROLL AND TUMBLE BLUES

as performed by Hambone Willie Newbern

Spanish Tuning: DGDGBD

(G⁷)

ALTERNATE FIRST FOUR BARS

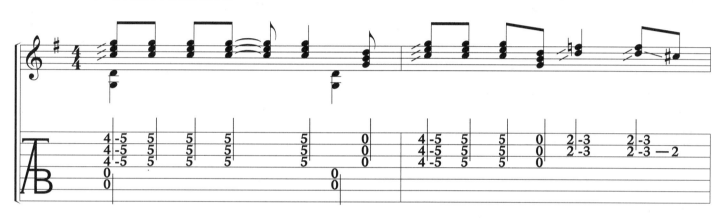

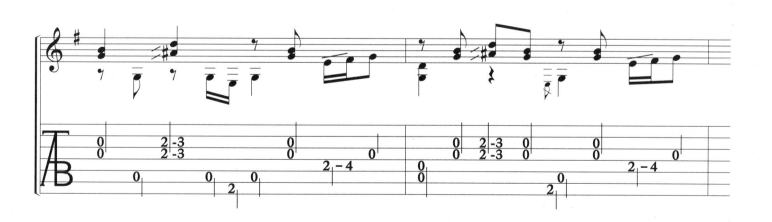

39

Roll and Tumble Blues

Lead Sheet

1. And I roll and I tumble and I cried the whole night long,
   And I roll and I tumble and I cried the whole night long,
   And I rose this morning, mama, and I didn't know right from wrong.

2. Did you ever wake up and find your dough roller gone,
   Did you ever wake up and find your dough roller gone,
   And your wring your head (and) you cry the whole day long.

3. And I told my woman just before I left the town,
   And I told my woman just before I left the town,
   Don't she let nobody tear her barrelhouse down.

4. And I fold my arms and I slowly walked away,
   And I fold my arms and I slowly walked away,
   Says that's alright, sweet mama, your trouble gonna come some day.

Charlie Patton

The archetypal first-generation Mississippi Delta bluesman, Charlie Patton was one of the country blues' most powerful artists. He spent most of his life in the heart of the Mississippi Delta on Dockery's vast plantation, where he helped shape the styles of Son House and Willie Brown, with whom he performed, as well as Robert Johnson, Howlin' Wolf, Pops Staples, and many others.

Patton was born during the 1880s in the country east of Jackson, Mississippi. In the true spirit of the blues, Patton is said to have taken up guitar as a relief from "women troubles." Charlie's first performing forays were into Bolton, where he was seen playing with members of the Chatman family, who later formed the Mississippi Sheiks. The Patton family moved north in 1897 and found work at Dockery's plantation. There Patton became enamored with the guitar playing of Henry Sloan. "Sloan was an old man who mostly just played chords," says blues scholar Gayle Dean Wardlow. "Patton was probably the first to do intricate rhythms and open tunings. Patton was already playing blues in 1909, so he developed his style before phonograph records were available." Another influence was older bluesman D. Irvin, who was remembered for his "guitar slapping" technique and performing stunts, which, according to Sam Chatmon, Patton made his own: "Charlie Patton was a clowning man with a guitar. He be in there putting his guitar all between his legs, carry it behind his head, lay down on the floor, and never stopped picking!"

The prolific Patton began recording for Paramount in June 1929, and by February 1934 had cut nearly 70 blues, folk, and gospel songs under his own name and appeared as a sideman on releases by Bertha Lee and Henry Sims. Patton's guitar approach made dramatic use of off-beat accenting, string snapping, hammer-ons, and percussive effects such as banging on the sound box. He was one of very few Delta bluesmen to play lap-style slide. Like Son House, Patton's voice was his most distinctive characteristic. Few people have ever sung with such conviction. Patton's gravel-rough voice often blurred the lyrics to the point of rendering them incomprehensible. As Son House observed, "You can be sitting right under him, and you can't hardly understand him."

A small, intense man who gravitated to drink and fight, Patton lived the hard life of a Mississippi sharecropper. He had many girlfriends, some of whom he was rumored to have beaten up, and fathered a number of children. Son House claimed that a heart condition had kept Patton out of the army during World War I. In 1930, Patton's throat was slit during an altercation; he survived but didn't record again for four years. Heavy drinking, heart problems, and other health issues caught up with him in 1934, when, not long after his comeback session, Charlie Patton passed away.

Charlie Patton recorded "Screamin' and Hollerin' the Blues" at his very first Paramount session, on June 14, 1929. Played in open-A tuning capoed up to B, the song demonstrates his string-snapping, guitar-body-slapping approach, and makes use of strong descending bass runs. Unlike the common AAB format, this one is ABC, and its stanzas are of uneven length. Lyrically, it bears similarities to Son House's earliest records.

Recording for Paramount, Charlie Patton cut his magnificent "Stone Pony Blues" in New York City on January 30, 1934. Like its predecessor, 1930's "Stone Pony," Patton played this one in standard tuning in the key of E with a capo. Patton vigorously finger-plucked the high-string leads near the end. Howlin' Wolf, who knew Patton, once demonstrated to John Hammond how Patton played the song: "At the end," Hammond recalled, "he flipped the guitar, which made three turns, caught it, and hit the last three notes! It was the most slick thing I've ever seen."

Another track from Charlie Patton's final session, "34 Blues" is essentially a remake of 1930's "Down the Dirt Road Blues." He played it in standard tuning and ended it with a nice solo flourish. Lyrically, the song is about Patton's being told to leave the Dockery Plantation where he'd spent much of his working life.

Screamin' and Hollerin' the Blues

as performed by Charlie Patton

Spanish Tuning: DGDGBD

INTRO (Pick-Up)

Note: X = Hit guitar and string together

1st VERSE

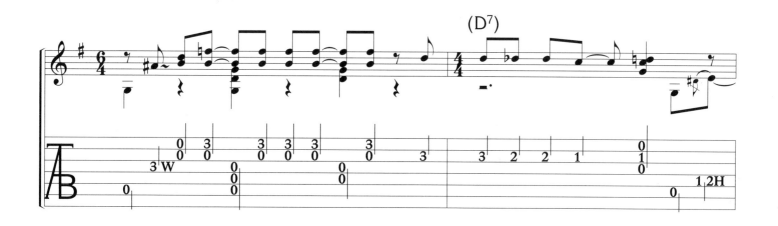

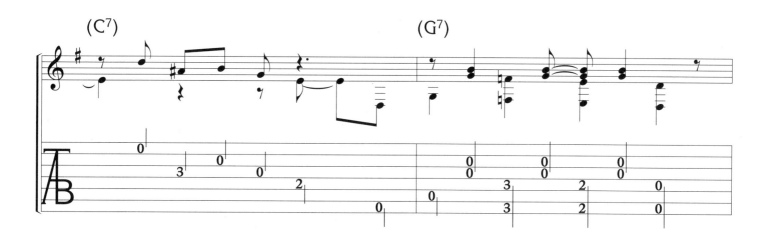

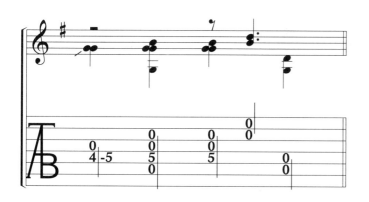

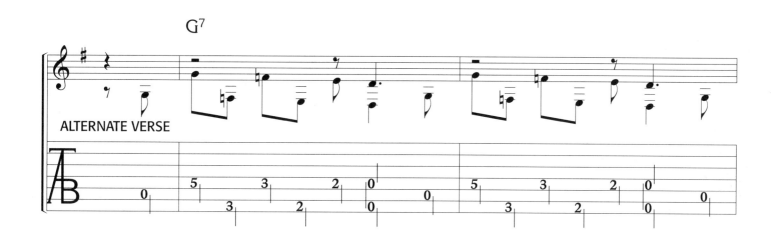

1st VARIATION—1st 4 BARS

to C Chord

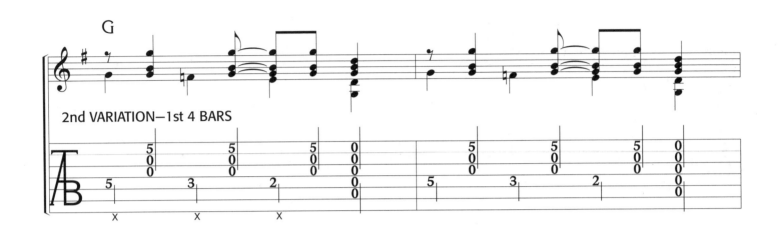

2nd VARIATION—1st 4 BARS

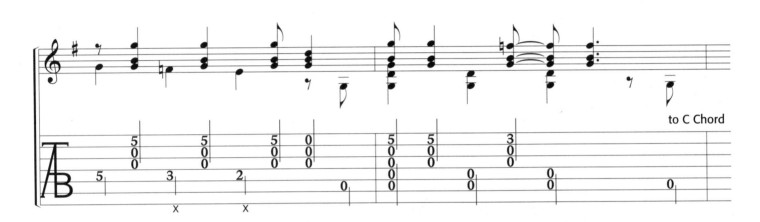

to C Chord

Screamin' and Hollerin' the Blues

Lead Sheet

1. Jackson on a high hill mama, Natchez just below,
   Jackson on a high hill mama, Natchez just beow,
   (Certain days you know how they are.)
   I ever get back home I won't be back no more.

2. For my mama's gettin' old, her head is turnin' grey.
   My mother's gettin' old, head is turnin' grey.
   Don't you know it'll break her heart know, my livin' this-a-way?

3. I woke up in the mornin', jinx all 'round your bed.
   If I woke up in the mornin', jinx all 'round your bed.
   (Children I know how it is, baby.)
   Turned my face to the wall an' I didn't have a word to say.

4. No use a-hollerin', no use a-screamin' and crying.
   No use a-hollerin', no use a-screamin' and crying.
   For you know you got a home, mama, long as I got mine.

5. Hey Lord have mercy on my wicked soul.
   Hey Lord have mercy on my wicked soul.
   (Baby you know I ain't gonna mistreat you.)
   I wouldn't mistreat you baby, for my weight in gold.

6. Oh I'm goin' away baby, don't you wanna go?
   I'm goin' away sweet mama, don't you wanna go?
   (I know you wanna go, baby.)
   Take God to tell when I'll be back here anymore.

Stone Pony Blues

as performed by Charlie Patton

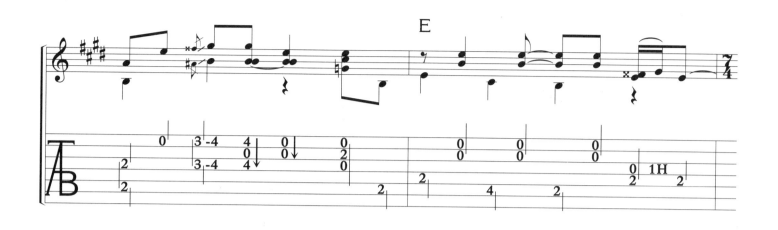

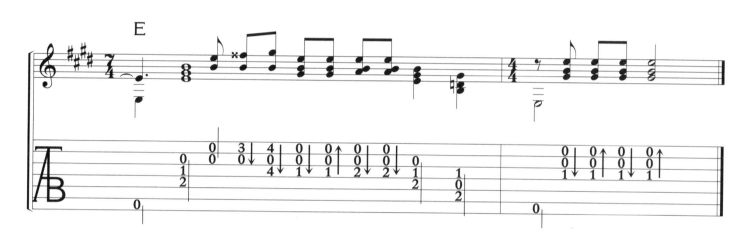

49

Stone Pony Blues

Lead Sheet

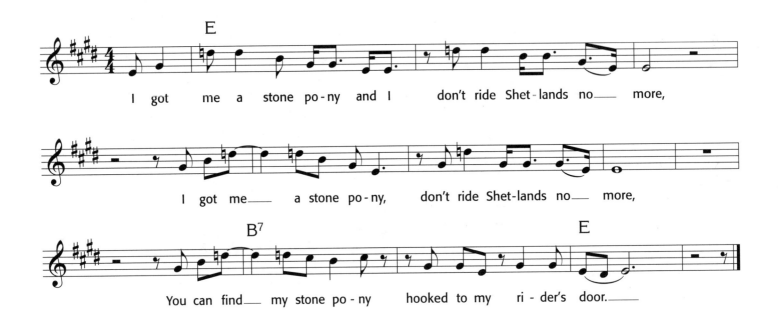

I got me a stone po-ny and I don't ride Shet-lands no__ more,

I got me__ a stone po-ny, don't ride Shet-lands no__ more,

You can find__ my stone po-ny hooked to my ri-der's door.__

1. I got me a stone pony and I don't ride Shetlands no more,
   I got me a stone pony, and I don't ride Shetlands no more,
   You can find my stone pony hooked to my rider's door.

2. Vicksburg's my pony, Rayville's my grey mare.
   Vicksburg's my pony, Rayville, Lord, is my grey mare.
   You can find my stone pony down in Louisiana town somewhere.

3. And I got me stone pony, don't ride Shetlands no more.
   Got a little stone pony, don't ride Shetlands no more.
   And I can't feel welcome, rider no where I go.

4. Vicksburg on a high hill and Natchez just below.
   Vicksburg on a high hill, Natchez just below.
   And I don't feel welcome, rider no where I go.

5. Well, I didn't come here, steal nobody's brown.
   Didn't come here to steal nobody's brown.
   I just stopped by here, well to keep you from stealin' mine.

6. Hello central, s'matter with your line.
   Hello central, s'matter now with your line.
   Come a storm last night and tore the wire down.

34 Blues

as performed by Charlie Patton

Standard Tuning

34 Blues

Lead Sheet

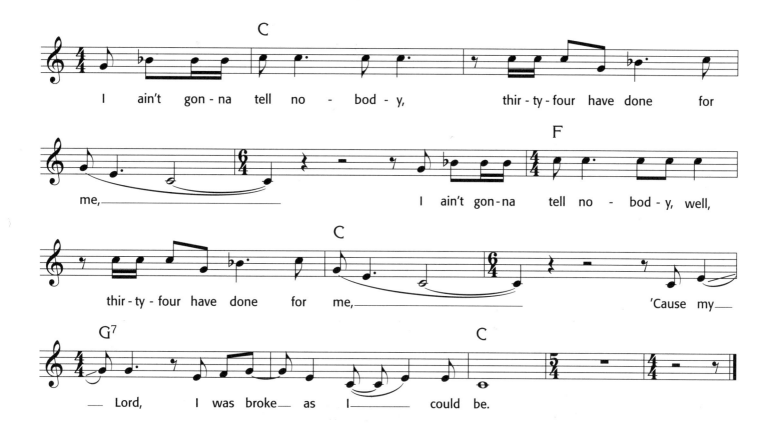

1. I ain't gonna tell nobody, thirty-four have done for me,
   I ain't gonna tell nobody, well, thirty-four have done for me,
   'Cause my Lord, I was broke as I could be.

2. They run me from Will Dockery's…
   They run me from Will Dockery's…
   (Buddy what's the matter).
   I went out an' told Papa Charlie,
   I don't want you hangin' 'round on my job no more.

3. Fella down in the country, it almost make you cry.
   Fella down in the country, it almost make you cry.
   (My God, chillun).
   Women and children flaggin' freight trains for rides.

4. Herman got a little six Buick, big six Chevrolet car.
   Herman got a little six Buick, little six Chevrolet car.
   (My God, what solid power).
   And it don't do nothin' but follow behind Holloway papa's plow.

5. And it may bring sorrow, Lord, it may bring tears.
   It may bring sorrow, Lord and it may bring tears.
   Oh Lord, oh Lord, let me see a brand new year.

ARTHUR PETTIS

"When the blues is telling you
You don't know what to do;
Ehh, you don't know what to do.
Imagine the one you love, now,
Them blues will soon leave you."
—Arthur Pettis, "Two Time Blues"

He was Arthur Petties when he first recorded in Memphis in 1928, but became Pettis on the records he made in Chicago just two years later. His recording career was brief and yielded only six titles, though Mississippi blues scholar Gayle Dean Wardlow asserts that Pettis made other recordings as Bill WIlliams, including duets with Sammy Sampson, who was in fact Big Bill Broonzy. The Broonzy connection is one of the few tangible threads in tracing Pettis. Paul Oliver wrote that Broonzy recalled Pettis hailed from "Big Bill's home district in Bolivar county...but had for many years been living in Chicago, and was still there."

In the liner notes of the Broonzy reissue, "Do That Guitar Rag" (Yazoo 1035), Stephen Calt and Woody Mann write of his "Big Bill Blues," "It has a similar structure to Arthur Petties' 'Out on Santa Fe Blues,' which is likewise played in the key of C and is probably indebted to Broonzy's work (or vice-versa)."

The Delta town of Tunica was Pettis' birthplace, but Wardlow believes he was already settled in Chicago by the time of his 1930 session there. There are rumors Pettis was shot, but nothing much for sure of him. We have only a handful of his recordings as evidence of his existence, but they're intriguing testaments. Though a Delta bluesman, Pettis occasionally tosses out "stop time" breaks in the manner of the southeastern ragtime players like Blind Blake. Wardlow hears a clear anticipation of Robert Johnson in some of Pettis' riffs, and others note the kingship to Broonzy's fluid playing. For all we might like to know of Arthur Pettis and many other biographical mysteries of the blues, we can at least know their music. Perhaps that's enough.

Good Boy Blues

by Arthur Pettis

Standard Tuning, capo 1

SKETCH of ACCOMPANIMENT to 1st VERSE

to 2nd Verse

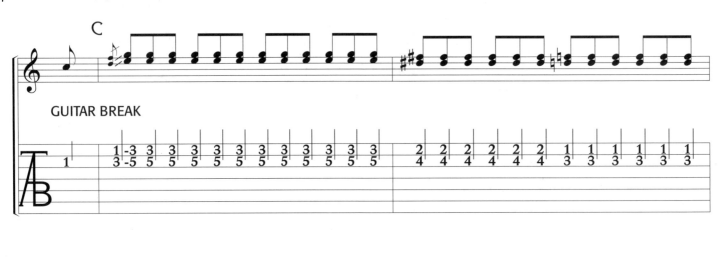

GUITAR BREAK

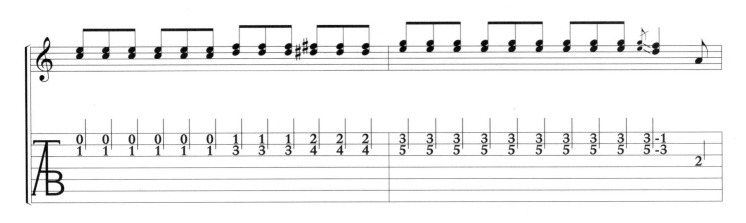

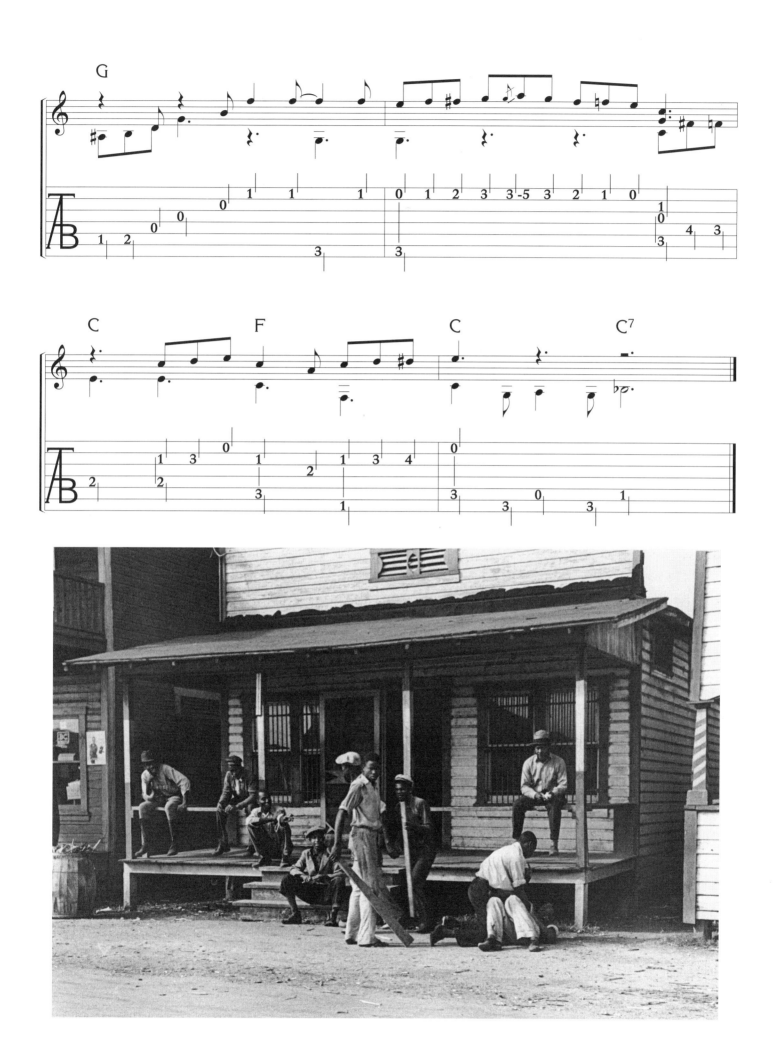

Good Boy Blues

Lead Sheet

1. When you's a good fella, they'll always leave you alone.
   When you's a good fella, they'll always leave you alone.
   When you's a bad fella, the jail will be your home.

2. Canned heat ain't no good boy, keep you with a flowery mind. [?]
   Canned heat ain't no good boy, keep you with a flowery mind. [?]
   So, just don't stir it open and you got a ramblin' mind.

3. You's sad and you worry, you looking through your mind.
   You's sad and you're wondering, you looking through your mind.
   So there's no more canned heat, when the judge gives you your time.

4. Wake up early morning, when everything must move.
   Wake up every morning, when everything must flow.
   'Cause the one you love, the blues will soon hit you.

5. Talking all night long, walking from place to place.
   Walking all night long, walking from place to place.
   I was wandering and walking, just to see my baby's face.

ROBERT WILKINS

"With my type of singing and playing, I believe I'd take the world if I was playing blues now. That's just the way I feel about it. But my conscience won't let me do it. But I really could play!"

—Rev. Robert Wilkins

In his 91 years, Robert Timothy Wilkins played many musical roles. He vividly recalled the Saturday night fish fries prior to World War I in his hometown of Hernanso, Mississippi, where he took up guitar at age 15 and soon became, he told Pete Welding, "mostly the leading songster and blues player there in Hernando." In the 1920s, "Tim" Wilkins would "bust music on the streets" of Memphis, and later proudly recalled playing for "the sporting class of people" in high-class brothels. Though no other recorded blues artist sounded quite like him, Wilkins claimed he tutored Memphis Minnie on guitar and taught Jim Jackson his biggest hit, "Kansas City Blues." For a man who later rejected blues as "songs of the evil spirit," Wilkins was not shy about trumpeting his accomplishments in the competitive Memphis blues scene of the 1920s and early '30s.

On the evidence of his surviving records from that era, his pride is justified. If Wilkins was neither prolific nor especially influential, he was nonetheless original as a blues composer and varied as a guitarist. His was an alternately light and powerful picking approach, and lyrics in Wilkins's blues tend to be cogent narratives rather than free-floating blues versus strung together, the common practice of country bluesmen. Recent blues commentary has frequently praised Wilkins's skills: Steve Calt called him "the rarest of blues commodities: a skilledsong designer... Wilkins trafficked in material that sounded bluesy but was not chiseled from the standard blues mold...His themes are thus different from each other in a way those of the typical bluesman are not." Comparing Wilkins to his Memphis contemporaries of the 1920s and '30s, Paul Oliver wrote: "His vocal range was greater, his tunes were more unusual, and his steady vocals with his use of sustained notes with deliberate vibrato were always the work of an intelligent, conscious artist."

Wilkins played blues for the last time in 1936. "I was playing a ball," Wilkins recalled three decades later, "and it just come to me to quit...it was just a sudden thing. Look like something appealed to me and I heard it: said, 'Don't do it anymore.' And I just hung it on the wall." Wilkins subsequently worked as a stockyard clerk, medicine salesman, and herbalist. In 1950, he became a minister in the Church of God of Christ, a black Pentecostal denomination in which foot washing, speaking in tongues, and spirited congregational singing hold sway. Religious music replaced the blues for Wilkins, who vigorously applied his secular talents to sacred themes. He put Sunday clothes on some of his old blues, replacing complaints of "lowdown women" with Biblical themes. This was the music Wilkins was playing when rediscovered in 1964. It has been called "holy blues," though the Rev. Robert Wilkins steadfastly asserted, "it don't say nothing in the Bible about playing any blues."

Ironically, the man whose debut recording in 1928 was "Rolling Stone, Parts I & II" would have one of his "holy blues" covered by the Rolling Stones on their 1968 *Beggars Banquet* album. "The Prodigal Son" was an epic "sermon in song" based upon the well-known parable which the Stones condensed from Wilkins's 22 verses to seven. The song used the tune of a 1929 Wilkins blues, "That's No Way to Get Along," which had a young man complaining to his mother of his abuse by "lowdown women." When Wilkins, living modestly in Memphis, was informed that one of the world's biggest rock bands had recorded "The Prodigal Son," he reportedly remarked, "Well, I'm just glad somebody liked my song well enough to record it."

THAT'S NO WAY TO GET ALONG

Open D Tuning: DADF#AD

That's No Way to Get Along

Lead Sheet

I'm goin' home,— friends sit down— and tell my,— my ma - ma,— my ma - ma;— Friends sit down and tell my ma,— I'm go - in' home, sit down and tell my ma; I'm go - in' home, sit down and tell my ma; That that's no way to get a - long.—

1. I'm goin' home, friends, sit down and tell
   my, my mama,
   Friends, sit down and tell my ma.
   I'm goin' home, sit down and tell my ma *(2x)*
   That that's no way to get along.

2. These low-down women, mama, they
   treated your, aw, poor son wrong,
   Mama, treated me wrong,
   These low-down women, mama, they
   treated your poor son wrong. *(2x)*
   And that's no way for him to get along.

3. They treated me like my poor heart was
   made of a rock or stone,
   Mama, made of a rock or stone.
   Treated me like my poor heart was made of
   a rock or stone. *(2x)*
   And that's no way for him to get along.

4. You know, that was enough, mama, to make
   your son wished he's dead and gone,
   Mama, wished I's dead and gone.
   That is enough to make your son, mama,
   wished he's dead and gone. *(2x)*
   'Cause that's no way for him to get along.

5. I stood on the roadside, I cried alone, all by
   myself, I cried alone by myself.
   I stood on the roadside and cried alone by
   myself. *(2x)*
   Cryin', "That's no way for me to get along."

6. I's wantin' some train to come along and take
   me away from here,
   Friends, take me 'way from here.
   Some train to come along and take me away
   from here. *(2x)*
   And that's no way for me to get along.